SAN FRANCISCO 49ERS

BY ALEX MONNIG

Published by The Child's World®
1980 Lookout Drive • Mankato, MN 56003-1705
800-599-READ • www.childsworld.com

Acknowledgments
The Child's World®: Mary Berendes, Publishing Director
Red Line Editorial: Editorial direction
The Design Lab: Design
Amnet: Production

Design Element: Dean Bertoncelj/Shutterstock Images
Photographs ©: Tony Gutierrez/AP Images, cover; Al
Messerschmidt Archive/AP Images, 5; Tom DiPace/AP
Images, 7; Paul Spinelli/AP Images, 9; Bettman/Corbis, 11, 17;
John Hefti/Icon Sportswire, 13, 21; Kevin Terrell/AP Images,
14-15, 25, 27; Gary Hershorn/Corbis, 19; Andy Kuno/
Corbis, 23; AP Images, 29

ISBN 9781634070164
LCCN 2014959721

Printed in the United States of America
PAO2345

ABOUT THE AUTHOR

Alex Monnig is a freelance journalist from St. Louis, Missouri, who now lives in Sydney, Australia. He has traveled across the world to cover sporting events in China, India, Singapore, New Zealand, and Scotland. No matter where he is, he always makes time to keep up to date with his favorite teams from his hometown.

TABLE OF CONTENTS

GO, 49ERS!

The San Francisco 49ers are one of the best teams in football history. They helped bring a new style of **offense** into the game. Their passing helped them become dominant. The 49ers were especially strong from 1981 to 1989. They won four championships in those nine years. Their fans have been packing the stands since 1946. Let's meet the 49ers.

49ers quarterback Joe Montana throws a pass during a 38–16 Super Bowl win over the Miami Dolphins on January 20, 1985.

WHO ARE THE 49ERS?

The San Francisco 49ers play in the National Football **League** (NFL). They are one of the 32 teams in the NFL. The NFL includes the American Football Conference (AFC) and the National Football Conference (NFC). The winner of the NFC plays the winner of the AFC in the Super Bowl. The 49ers play in the West Division of the NFC. The 49ers have won five Super Bowls. Only the Pittsburgh Steelers have won more. The 49ers have also scored the second most Super Bowl points.

The 49ers scored 49 points against the San Diego Chargers in the Super Bowl after the 1994 season.

WHERE THEY CAME FROM

The 49ers entered the NFL in 1950. They made the playoffs only four times in their first 31 years. Coach Bill Walsh took over in 1979. He introduced the West Coast Offense. It involves short passes across the field. Many teams use the West Coast Offense today. The 49ers won three Super Bowls under Walsh. George Seifert took over in 1989. San Francisco won two titles under Seifert. The 49ers won at least ten games each season from 1983 to 1998.

Bill Walsh was one of the most successful coaches in 49ers history.

WHO THEY PLAY

The 49ers play 16 games each season. With so few games, each one is important. Every year, the 49ers play two games against each of the other three teams in their division. The Arizona Cardinals, Seattle Seahawks, and St. Louis Rams are also in the NFC West. They are **rivals** of the 49ers. The Rams used to play in Los Angeles. Now they play in St. Louis. They are the only team the 49ers have played every season. The New York Giants are another rival. They played the 49ers in the playoffs six times from 1981 to 1993.

49ers fullback Joe Perry (34) gets tripped up during a 23–14 loss to the Los Angeles Rams on September 26, 1955.

WHERE THEY PLAY

The 49ers play in Levi's Stadium. It opened in 2014. It holds more than 70,000 fans. The stadium also has a 49ers museum. The 49ers lost the first regular season game there. But fans expect to see more wins in years to come. The 49ers used to play in Candlestick Park. They shared it with the city's baseball team until 2000. That meant there was dirt from the baseball diamond on the field when the 49ers played.

Fire shoots into the air before a game against the Kansas City Chiefs at Levi's Stadium on October 5, 2014.

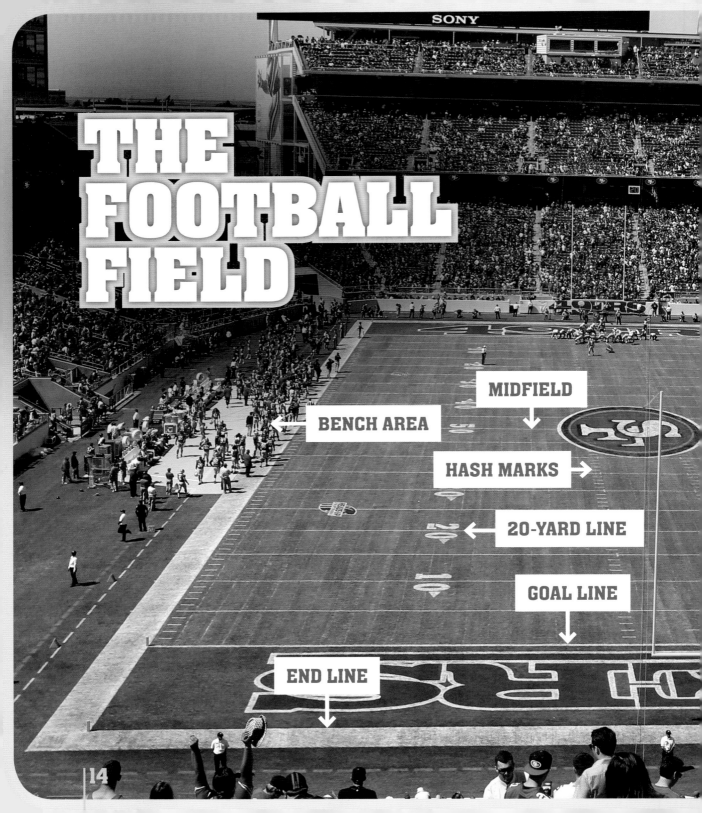

THE FOOTBALL FIELD

MIDFIELD

BENCH AREA

HASH MARKS

20-YARD LINE

GOAL LINE

END LINE

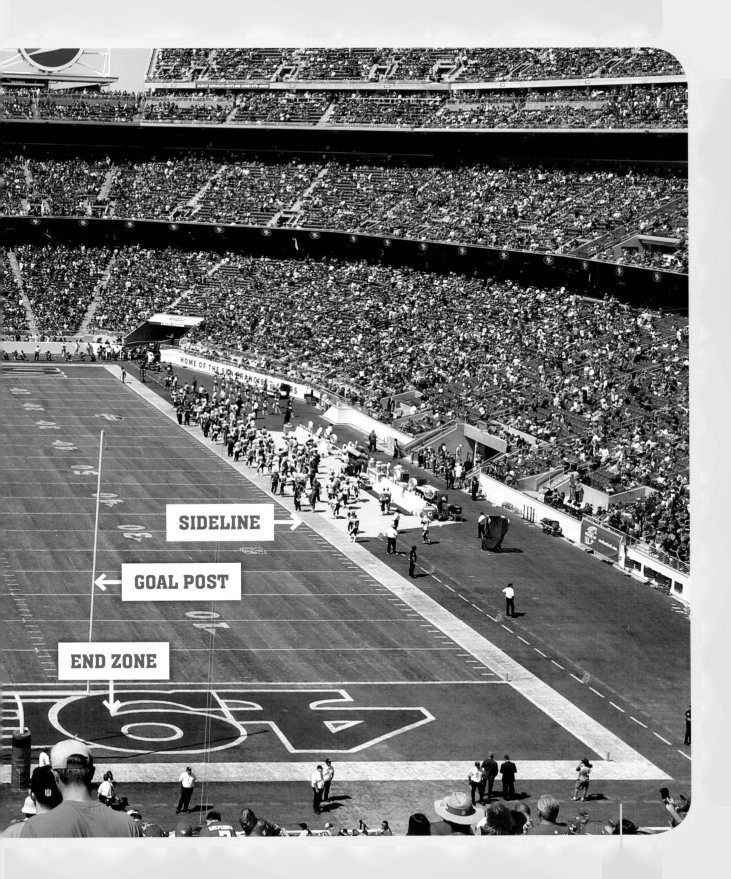

SIDELINE

GOAL POST

END ZONE

BIG DAYS

The 49ers have had some great moments in their history. Here are three of the greatest:

1979—San Francisco chose quarterback Joe Montana in the NFL Draft. They picked him with the last pick of the third round. He became one of the best quarterbacks ever. The 49ers won four Super Bowls with him.

1982—The 49ers trailed the Dallas Cowboys 27-21 in the NFC Championship Game on January 10. There were 51 seconds left. Montana took the snap. He was under pressure. He threw the ball to the back corner of the **end zone**. Nobody was there. Then wide receiver Dwight Clark came out of nowhere to make "The Catch." The 49ers won 28-27. They went on to win their first Super Bowl.

49ers wide receiver Dwight Clark (87) leaps to make the game-winning catch against the Dallas Cowboys in the NFC Championship Game on January 10, 1982.

1990—On January 28, San Francisco won its fourth Super Bowl. It was its second in a row. The 49ers destroyed the Denver Broncos 55-10. That is a record for points scored in a Super Bowl through 2014.

TOUGH DAYS

Football is a hard game. Even the best teams have rough games and seasons. Here are some of the toughest times in 49ers history.

1991—The 49ers were going for their third Super Bowl in a row after the 1990 season. But they lost to the New York Giants in the NFC Championship Game. Joe Montana was injured in the fourth quarter. He missed the entire next season. He missed most of the 1992 season, too. He never started another game for the 49ers.

1999—San Francisco had won at least ten games each season from 1983 to 1998. Quarterbacks Montana and Steve Young had led the team. But Montana was gone. Young played only three games due to injuries. He retired that season. All that added up to a 4-12 record.

Half the lights went out in the stadium during San Francisco's 34–31 loss to the Baltimore Ravens in the Super Bowl on February 3, 2013.

2013—Fans of the 49ers had never seen their team lose the Super Bowl. But the 49ers lost to the Baltimore Ravens on February 3. The lights went out for 34 minutes early in the second half. San Francisco was down 28–6 at the time. They fought back. But the Ravens held on to win 34–31.

MEET THE FANS

The 49ers often make the playoffs. Fans pack the home stadium in the fall and winter months. Mascot Sourdough Sam gets fans riled up. He is an old gold miner. That is because "49ers" is a nickname for people who came to California during the Gold Rush starting in 1849.

49ers fans in red and white erupt after a touchdown pass at Levi's Stadium on October 5, 2014.

HEROES THEN

Joe Montana and Steve Young are two of the best quarterbacks ever. Both are Pro Football Hall of Famers. They made 15 **Pro Bowls** combined. They won two **Most Valuable Player (MVP)** awards each. Both got to throw to wide receiver Jerry Rice. Rice was one of the best football players ever. Rice made 12 Pro Bowls with the 49ers. Through 2014, he has more career catches (1,549), receiving yards (22,895), and receiving **touchdowns** (197) than any player ever. Most of those came with the 49ers. Ronnie Lott was the defensive leader from 1981 to 1990. He was a hard hitter. He also made interceptions. He made the Pro Bowl every year with the 49ers except one.

Wide receiver Jerry Rice had 187 touchdowns with the 49ers.

HEROES NOW

Colin Kaepernick became the 49ers' starting quarterback during the 2012 season. Some fans questioned if he could be a star. He quickly proved he was. That year he led the team to the Super Bowl. Kaepernick is dangerous because he is a good passer but also a speedy runner. Defenders have to be ready for both. Defensive linemen Aldon Smith and Justin Smith are fast and strong. When they charge into the backfield, opposing quarterbacks have little time to make plays.

49ers quarterback Colin Kaepernick runs with the ball against the Arizona Cardinals on December 28, 2014.

GEARING UP

NFL players wear team uniforms. They wear helmets and pads to keep them safe. Cleats help them make quick moves and run fast. Some players wear extra gear for protection.

THE FOOTBALL

NFL footballs are made of leather. Under the leather is a lining that fills with air to give the ball its shape. The leather has bumps or "pebbles." These help players grip the ball. Plastic laces help players control their throws. Footballs are also called "pigskins" because some of the first balls were made from pig bladders. Today they are made of leather from cows.

49ers linebacker Aldon Smith lines up before a play against the St. Louis Rams on December 8, 2013.

HELMET

SHOULDER PADS

THIGH PADS

GLOVES

FOOTBALL

SPORTS STATS

ere are some of the all-time career records for the San Francisco 49ers. All the stats are through the 2014 season.

PASSING YARDS

Joe Montana 35,124

John Brodie 31,548

RUSHING YARDS

Frank Gore 11,073

Joe Perry 8,689

RECEPTIONS

Jerry Rice 1,281

Terrell Owens 592

TOTAL TOUCHDOWNS

Jerry Rice 187

Terrell Owens 83

SACKS

Bryant Young 89.5

Charles Haley 66.5

POINTS

Jerry Rice 1,130

Ray Wersching 979

49ers safety Ronnie Lott (42) jumps for an interception against the Los Angeles Raiders on September 22, 1985.

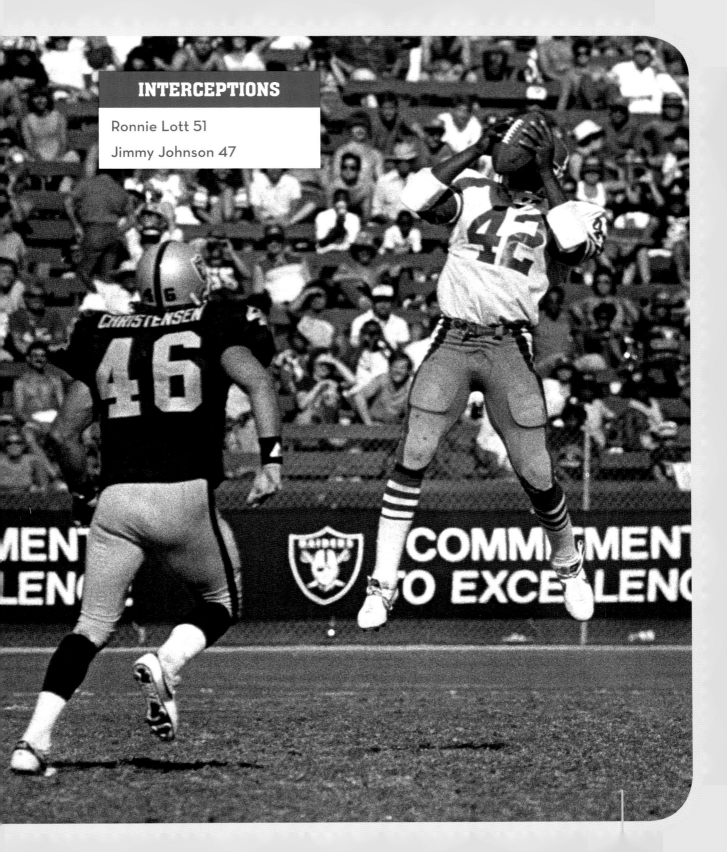

INTERCEPTIONS

Ronnie Lott 51

Jimmy Johnson 47

GLOSSARY

end zone section on either end of the field that players must reach in order to score a touchdown

league an organization of sports teams that compete against each other

Most Valuable Player (MVP) a yearly award given to the top player in the NFL

offense when a team has the ball and is trying to score

Pro Bowl the NFL's all-star game where the best players in the league compete

rivals teams whose games bring out the greatest emotion between the players and the fans on both sides

touchdowns methods of scoring worth six points in which a player has control of the ball in the other team's end zone

FIND OUT MORE

IN THE LIBRARY

Brown, Daniel. *100 Things 49ers Fans Should Know & Do Before They Die*. Chicago: Triumph Books, 2013.

Editors of Sports Illustrated Kids.
Sports Illustrated Kids Football: Then to Wow!
New York: Time Home Entertainment, 2014.

Garner, Joe, and Bob Costas. *100 Yards of Glory: The Greatest Moments in NFL History*.
New York: Houghton Mifflin Harcourt, 2011.

Maiocco, Matt. *San Francisco 49ers: The Complete Illustrated History*. Minneapolis, MN: MBI, 2013.

ON THE WEB

Visit our Web site for links about the San Francisco 49ers:
childsworld.com/links

Note to Parents, Teachers, and Librarians: We routinely verify our Web links to make sure they are safe and active sites. So encourage your readers to check them out!

INDEX